Channels of Devotion

Channels
of
Devotion

Twenty-four Story Worship Services

Gladys C. Murrell

A B I N G D O N   P R E S S
NEW YORK   •   NASHVILLE

CHANNELS OF DEVOTION

Copyright MCMXLVIII by Stone & Pierce

Library of Congress Catalog Card Number: 48-3682

SET UP, PRINTED, AND BOUND BY THE
PARTHENON PRESS, AT NASHVILLE,
TENNESSEE, UNITED STATES OF AMERICA

DEDICATED TO

*my beloved companion through the years
and to
all good comrades of "The Way"*

Preface

THESE WORSHIP SERVICES HAVE BEEN PREPARED IN
response to a need for devotional programs, twenty to
thirty minutes in length, which can be given with a
minimum amount of preparation on the part of the
leader. They may be extended in time by vocal or
instrumental music on the theme of the service. The
story may be read or told.

These services are helpful when several persons
participate in the various readings. The effectiveness
of a worship service in which each takes part at the
proper time without introduction is well known. However, the leader may present the entire service if that
is desired.

Youth and adult groups in the church were kept
especially in mind in the planning of this book, but
the services may be used also in morning watch,
vespers, and opening or closing worship services of
other organizations. Several of these services have been
used successfully in Y.W.C.A., P.T.A., and business
women's groups and in retreats, summer camps, and
schools, as well as in church organization meetings.

GLADYS C. MURRELL

Contents

Answered Prayer

This flesh is but the symbol and the shrine
Of an immense and unimagined beauty,
Not mortal but divine.
—ANGELA MORGAN [1]

SCRIPTURE: Proverbs 3:1-6.

HYMN: "Guide Me, O Thou Great Jehovah."

THE STORY:

Nearly five hundred years ago a motherless girl named Mary lived in the country near Florence, Italy. Her father was a vinedresser and she kept his small cottage neat and cooked his simple fare. Near by in a hut lived an old hermit whose greatest comfort was a large spreading tree, in the shade of which he spent his days. Mary often brought him a bowl of porridge, and as she was the only one who seemed to care for him, he grew very fond of her.

Each time she brought him food and swept out his small hut, the old man prayed: "May this sheltering tree and the girl Mary be blessed and remembered to the end of time." Because he prayed, he did not doubt that God would grant his request.

The months and years passed by and the old hermit died. Mary's father too passed away and the sheltering

11

tree was felled by lightning. The girl married a charcoal maker and became the mother of two lovely children. One day as she sat at the window of her little
home some gentlemen from Florence strolled by. One
of them was the great artist Raphael on a holiday. He
carried no canvas or paints, but when he saw Mary
with her young babe in her arms and the small child at
her knee, he knew he must capture the beauty of that
moment.

Picking up the head of a cask and plucking a stick
of charcoal from the smoldering fire, he asked her to
remain as she was. Quickly he sketched the young
mother and the children, fitting the drawing into the
circle of the cask head. Then after thanking her he
returned to his studio, where he painted an immortal
picture. He did not know that the cask head had been
made of the old tree that sheltered the hermit or that
he had helped to answer the prayer of the old man,
that the girl Mary and the tree be blessed and remembered to the end of time. Indeed he did not know her
story but the "Madonna of the Chair" by Raphael is
probably the best-loved picture in the world.

ANSWERED PRAYER

I asked for bread; God gave a stone instead.
Yet, while I pillowed there my weary head,
    The angels made a ladder of my dreams,
Which upward to celestial mountains led.
    And when I woke beneath the morning's beams,
Around my resting place fresh manna lay;
And, praising God, I went upon my way.
        For I was fed.

God answers prayer; sometimes, when hearts are weak,
He gives the very gifts believers seek.
   But often faith must learn a deeper rest,
And trust God's silence when he does not speak;
   For he whose name is Love will send the best.
Stars may burn out, nor mountain walls endure,
But God is true, his promises are sure
       For those who seek.

—MYRA GOODWIN PLANTZ

PRAYER:

Father, we thank thee for the great ideas of our
nature, and the revelation and inspiration which thou
dost give thy children, working in the human soul,
and for human souls that are obedient unto thee. We
remember our daily lives before thee, and we sorrow
that with so great opportunities we have not used the
fullness of them. May our lives be squared by the
Golden Rule so that all who come in contact shall
be blessed. Amen.

Appreciation of Other Races

Dreams are they—but they are God's dreams!
Shall we decry them and scorn them?
That men shall love one another,
That white shall call black man brother,
That greed shall pass from the market-place,
That lust shall yield to love for the race,
That men shall meet with God face to face—
Dreams are they all,
    But shall we despise them—
    God's dreams!

—THOMAS CURTIS CLARK [3]

SCRIPTURE: I Peter 3:8-13; II Peter 1:3-11.

HYMNS: "Where Cross the Crowded Ways of Life";
"We Bear the Strain of Earthly Care."

THE STORY:

When a city church was built there was need for a huge stained-glass window to grace the most conspicuous wall of the sanctuary. Many famous artists competed for the privilege of designing the window, but the drawing which most pleased the committee was submitted by an unknown artist. He received a letter notifying him that his design entitled "The Place Where the Young Child Lay" was accepted. He was

14

commissioned to have the window made in time to be dedicated on Christmas Eve.

Now the unknown artist bore a grudge because he felt he had been discriminated against on account of his dark skin, and he kept himself secluded in his attic studio. This opportunity to design a window for the beautiful and stately Church of the Redeemer gave him a chance to work out his grudge.

On the morning it happened that his wife had been hanging out the family washing and had come in wearing a shawl over her head and carrying the baby in a basket. She leaned over as she placed the basket on a chair.

"Stay just as you are," called her husband, "imagine the basket is the manger and that you are Mary, the mother of Jesus."

So she kept the pose and he painted her. It was far lovelier than he had planned, because in the heart of his wife was none of the bitter grudge which he harbored.

After days of labor the masterpiece was finished and ready for the stained-glass factory workers. The week before Christmas, when the trained men were assembling the bits of glass, neither the face nor the arms of the Madonna could be found. Finally the artist arrived with them, saying it was his whim to place them himself.

After the workmen had gone he fastened in place the lovely brooding face of the Madonna, her arms hovering over the wee child.

At the dedication of the window the artist sat in a back pew. He saw the consternation of the people as they looked at his window. A whisper went around:

"The face of the Madonna is black! A black Madonna in the Church of the Redeemer!"

The artist quietly chuckled to himself and felt repaid for his own suffering.

The news of the window was telephoned over town and on Christmas day the church was crowded. Now the minister of the church was a good man, a just man, a gentleman. He had lain awake all night wondering how he was going to preach from the text: "In him was life; and the life was the light of men." He had meant to base his sermon on the Madonna window.

As he entered the sanctuary he found it full of people gazing curiously at the masterpiece.

"Lord help me to find the right words to say," he prayed silently. Then as he began his sermon the winter sun blazed through the window with the extra dazzle of a snowy day. As its beams came breaking through the stained glass, a gasp of sheer surprise spread through the church; for in that blaze of sunshine, the Madonna's face was shining, pure as an angel. The little Christ child was a sheen of dazzling glory. Inspired by the miracle of the transfigured Madonna, the minister preached a sermon that marked a milestone in the life of every person present. He closed with these words: "In deep humility I have spoken this Christmas Day. Last evening when the Saviour looked down into this church, who really looked black to his all-seeing gaze—the black Madonna or you and I, with our black consternation? The curious blackness of our hearts could not see God shine through a face of another color. Let us, then, this Christmas morning be wise men bringing gifts to the Saviour of all mankind; and in the place where the young child lay, let us place the most difficult present to give up—our race prejudice."

The artist then rose and, walking slowly to the pulpit, placed in the minister's hand a package. Haltingly he spoke: "This is my Christmas present to this church which I have wronged. See, here is the original glass which you ordered for the face of the Madonna and child. The other glass I made myself. Your minister has shown me that I too am color blind. But I have seen this morning that there is neither black nor white when the light of God shines through. Tomorrow I will change the face of the Madonna. Today I will give a gift of my grudge and hate to the Saviour. I am ashamed."

Then the chairman of the official board arose: "We too have learned a lesson! Let us leave the black Madonna in its place forever, that our children and our children's children may witness the miracle as the light of God shines through our Madonna window."

Then there was a hush and a voice in the choir softly sang these words from a Christmas carol:

> How silently, how silently,
>   The wondrous gift is given!
> So God imparts to human hearts
>   The blessings of His heaven.
> No ear may hear His coming
>   But in this world of sin,
> Where meek souls will receive Him still
>   The dear Christ enters in.[3]

THE RACES OF THE EARTH

Who is that dare say that one race stands
Superior to another—that God's hands

Moved favorably for one, and not another?
Who can say: "This one man is my brother,
And not that one?" The black men think of Christ
As black of skin. To them he has sufficed
As Saviour, and the yellow race may claim
A yellow Jesus with a Chinese name,
While he, the Father of us all looks down
Upon each land, the country and the town
And sees his children, and he loves us all.
Who am I to stand aloof, and call
My brother or my sister less than I?
We are one family here beneath God's sky,
With one Father and one heavenly home above.
Lord, help us reach all races with our love!

—GRACE NOLL CROWELL [4]

PRAYER:

Forgive, O Lord, our severing ways,
The rival altars that we raise,
The wrangling tongues that mar Thy praise!

Thy grace impart! In time to be
Shall one great temple rise to Thee—
Thy Church our broad humanity.

White flowers of love its walls shall climb,
Soft bells of peace shall ring its chime,
Its days shall all be holy time.

A sweeter song shall then be heard,
Confessing, in a world's accord.
The inward Christ, the living Word.

That song shall swell from shore to shore,
One hope, one faith, one love restore
The seamless robe that Jesus wore. Amen.

—JOHN GREENLEAF WHITTIER

Brotherhood

The world is full of children
  Of many different ways.
Some are used to icebergs,
  And some to torrid days;
Some have tassels, some have beads,
  Some have fan or feather.
What a joyful time they'd have
  If they got together!

The world is full of children
  Of many different kinds,
And many different costumes,
  And many different minds;
Some in silk and some in fur,
  And some in cloth or leather;
But if they had a half a chance
  They'd like to play together.
—Nancy Byrd Turner [5]

Scripture: Luke 13:22-30; Micah 4:3-5.

Hymn: "Jesus Calls Us, O'er the Tumult."

The Story:

In a little-known part of our great earth there is a beautiful garden where love reigns. Here men, women, and children live in perfect fellowship and each performs the tasks suited to his ability. None feels himself superior to another.

19

Here people of all races bring their various gifts to their king, who lives in the garden, knowing that he, who rules them with love, will cause the humblest offering to glow with radiant beauty.

Many who do not live in the garden gaze through the tall white gate with longing. The wall is too high to climb and one can enter only through the gate called "Peace." No gatekeeper bars the way, but the gate has a strange and wonderful lock.

A man, whose skin was white, once brought a metal key of great beauty and intricate design. He pushed others aside to try the key, but being unsuccessful in opening the lock went sadly away.

Then came one of yellow skin who held secretively in his flowing sleeve a key exquisitely carved of jade. He hoped none might guess his errand, but he too departed in sorrow.

Then a man of brown skin tried a key of ebony. It was curiously shaped and inlaid with pearl. He carried it proudly and confidently, but the lock did not open.

A black-skinned man arrived stealthily, with a key shaped from an ivory tusk. He had learned that all men were not his friends. Although he worked patiently, he was forced to leave the gate unopened.

Lastly came a man of red skin, with a key that was shaped like an arrow. In no way did it fit the lock of the gate.

At length one day all these men met near the gate called "Peace"—men of red, black, brown, white, and yellow skins. The eye of each sought the one he feared most.

Slowly and cautiously each man crept toward the

gate. As one would almost reach it, another would trip him or push him away. Each was afraid the other would gain entrance to the garden closing the door upon the rest.

On that day the king's son was walking in the garden. As he drew near the gate he sensed the tragedy of selfish men pushing others back from the fulfillment of their dreams.

"Have you not learned, my brothers of the earth," he said, "that you must find a way to come into this garden together? None of you has the power to come alone through the gate called 'Peace.' The garden is lovelier than ever you have dreamed. Come now, my brothers, together find the way. But I will tell you this: the key which opens this gate must be forged of service, tolerance, trust, co-operation, and faith."

As the king's son finished speaking he gazed at them lovingly and hopefully. Then he passed on.

The white man looked at his key and saw that it was service. He laid it in the palm of the yellow man, whose key was co-operation. Astonishingly, the two keys became one. The yellow man joined it to the key of tolerance, held by the brown man. The metal, jade, and ebony keys fused into a single one of great beauty. Wonderingly, the brown man handed the precious object to the black man, whose key was trust, and before their eyes these also became one. The final miracle was accomplished when the arrow of faith was added by the red man and the key shone with a light not of this world.

"Who shall turn the key to open the gate called 'Peace'?" the men asked, together. None felt worthy and each pressed the privilege upon the other.

Then a strange thing happened. They key itself moved from hand to hand, joining their fingers tightly, and together they went forward. The gate of peace swung open as if by magic.

The brown, the white, the red, the black, and the yellow ran laughing like brothers into the garden to live forever.

The king of the garden counted the key which opened the way as his most precious possession, for it meant that his earthly children had learned a lesson of life which he and his son had known from the beginning of time.

> Why do I dare love all mankind?
> 'Tis not because each face, each form
> Is comely, for it is not so;
> Nor is it that each soul is warm
> With Godlike glow.
> Yet there's no one to whom's not given
> Some little lineament of heaven,
> Some partial symbol, at the least, or sign
> Of what should be, if it is not, within
> Reminding of the life of the Divine.
> —H. B. SUTTON

PRAYER:

Our loving Father, we come to thee in the name of him in whom thou art revealed, who gave his loving service to men of all races, and who helped the stranger, the unloved, the unlovely, even as he served his disciples. Deepen our respect for other peoples, enlarge our understanding, and transcend our differences.

Cleanse all our hearts from our disgrace—
    We love not world but clan;
Make clear our eyes to see our race
    One family of man.

Rend thou our little temple veils
    That cloak the truth divine,
Until thy mighty word prevails
    That cries, "All souls are mine." Amen.
                —HARRY EMERSON FOSDICK [6]

Christmas

A king might miss the guiding star,
  A wise man's foot might stumble;
For Bethlehem is very far
  From all except the humble.
                    —Louis Benson [7]

Scripture: Luke 2:1-20.

Hymns: "O Little Town of Bethlehem"; "Silent
Night"; "We Would See Jesus."

I shall go tonight on a pilgrimage
  To Bethlehem's manger lowly;
I shall gaze on a mother's wistful smile
  And worship the Christ child holy.

As shepherds of old left their flocks at night
  I shall leave my worries and care;
As the wise men brought Him their choicest gifts
  I shall offer Him homage fair.

My myrrh will be faith and humility,
  The gold, my talents and pence,
And a hopeful heart filled with love toward all
  Will be my frankincense.
                    —Ruth Carwell Kespohl [8]

When God wants an important thing done in this
world or a wrong righted, he goes about it in a very
singular way. He does not release his thunderbolts or
stir up earthquakes. He simply has a tiny baby born,
24

perhaps in a humble home, of a very humble mother. But
he puts the idea or purpose into the mother's heart. And
she puts it into the baby's mind; and then—God waits!

The great events of this world are not battles and
elections and earthquakes and thunderbolts. The great
events are babies; for each child comes as a possible savior
with the message that God is not discouraged of man, but
is still expecting to become incarnate in each human life.
—EDWARD McDONALD [9]

THE STORY:

Like the curtains of a sanctuary the shadowy twilight of a winter's evening gathered around the village
of Bethlehem. As the shadows deepened, lights were
kindled one by one in the windows of whitewashed
houses. Toward the north, the south, and the east, the
slopes of the hill were trimly terraced in gardens, vineyards, and orchards of olive, lemon, citron, almond, and
pomegranate.

On the eastern slope, somewhat below the town, a
man was still busily working in his orchard. Among his
neighbors he was known as a prudent, thrifty, and
successful husbandman, the owner of several of the
most fruitful vineyards and gardens. His name was
Ben David. He had just dismissed a score of laborers
who had been helping him gather the harvest of citrons
and lemons which ripen in December, and now he
stood for a moment gazing back at the well-kept
orchard and then out over the fields of the shepherds
and on into the east, where the reflection of the sunset
still lingered upon the heights of Moab, in wondrous
tints of purple and of lavender. He murmured to himself: "I do not think enough of these things. I am too
much occupied with the gardens and the orchards. I

must not lose the things that are most worth while."

Turning quickly he mounted the hill toward the town, passed in through the eastern gate, and soon found his own substantial house bordering the main road of the village. There he devoured with healthy appetite the evening meal which the servants set before him, and going out into the quiet night he sat down on the steps of the house and began to figure the value of the crop of citrons and lemons which was being gathered. It had been a good season for the orchards. He was so absorbed in this calculation that he did not hear the laughter of children playing in the streets, nor did he notice the frequent passage of neighbors and friends before the door. Suddenly, however, he was aware that a group of persons had stopped before his house, and looking up he saw the bent form of a woman sitting wearily upon a patient little beast, while the man who was her attendant had approached the steps of the house, and, lifting a noble face upon which anxiety was written, he asked if they might find lodging for the night. They had visited the inn, he explained, and it was overcrowded. The wife was weary and ill, and they needed refuge.

Now Ben David was not a hardhearted man, but he had lived primarily for himself. He knew there were rooms in his spacious house that, with a little attention from the servants, might be made ready for these guests, but it would involve obligations of courtesy on his part, which just then he felt he was too busy to undertake. After a momen'ts reflection he answered, not unkindly but not altogether truly, that he had no room to spare.

Just then the woman lifted her face, which had been

muffled in her garments. The light of the open door
fell full upon it. It was a countenance on which purity
and pain were mingled in a wondrous way. In it there
seemed to be such depth of yearning and wistful appeal
that it made upon Ben David a distinct and indelible
impression—so much so that he was about to change
his mind. But it was too late. The man had descended
the steps, and the little group had passed on into the
darkness of the unlighted street.

Ben David rose, entered the house, and somewhat
impatiently bade the servant unroll his sleeping mat
upon the floor. He was vexed with himself and could
not sleep. As the night wore on he heard without in
the street the hurried steps of men and the murmur of
their voices, vibrant with suppressed excitement. Ris-
ing, he went to the window, and looking out he saw
the familiar forms of several shepherds who kept their
flocks in the fields below his orchards. One man paused
long enough to tell him a story almost too strange to be
true.

"Tonight," he said, "as we watched our flocks,
drowsing about the fire, the starry heavens above us
seemed to burst into blossom like a rose, and out of the
pulsing heart of it there fell the music of celestial
voices, telling us of a wondrous child who had been
born this night in Bethlehem, whose coming would
be glad tidings of great joy to all people." Under the
spell of the vision, he said, they hastened to the town.
Searching everywhere, they saw at last a light burning
dimly in the rock-cut stable of the Khan of Chimham,
and there, lying in the straw among the wakeful cattle,
they had found the mother and the wondrous child.
They had been too amazed to speak at first, but now,

returning, their tongues were loosed, and they were glorifying God for all the things which they had seen and heard.

When the man had gone Ben David stood a long time at the window wondering at the things which had been told him by the shepherds. He remembered all the wistful hopes and dreams which centered about the mystical figure of the Messiah. Was this indeed the long-expected king? In the morning he would find the child. Returning to his bed, he slept until the gray dawn crept reverently in through the windows as if the day were on its knees.

Ben David rose softly, for the vision of the night was still upon him, but he remembered also the harvest of citrons and lemons which was not fully gathered. The laborers would be waiting for his instructions, the merchant would be on hand to bargain for the crop, and he must hasten his steps; but in the evening he would surely take time to find the child.

So the days passed into weeks and the weeks slipped into months and the spring had come, vibrant with the song of birds and heavy with the fragrance of flowers. Ben David sat again on the steps of his house in the cool of the evening. He was figuring the almond harvest which promised to be so abundant. He was thinking of the gold that would be offered for his crop, and the new vineyard which would be purchased with the money.

As he sat there he heard the silver tinkle of camel bells coming in through the eastern gate, and the shuffling tread of heavy beasts and the clank of swords and ornaments. He could scarcely believe his eyes, for here came three stately men with snowy hair and long white beards who sat high on swinging camels decked with crimson cloths. Three kings they surely were, for they were clothed in purple and fine linen. Ben David salaamed with great respect, and descending to the street he plucked one of the attendants by the coat and said: "Peace be unto you, sir. Who may these three kings be and what high mission brings them to our humble village?" Before the man could reply, one of the stately strangers, bending from his camel, said to the Bethlehemite: "Good sir, can you tell us where is he that is born king of the Jews, for we have seen his star in the east and are come to worship him?" Then pointing with the finger, he directed his gaze toward the brilliant star which seemed to hang like a silver lamp over the caravansary of Chimham.

"Ah," said Ben David, as memory stirred within him, "it must be the child you seek."

"Yes," said the stranger, "it is the child—the royal child."

"Then," said Ben David, "you will find him yonder," and he directed their steps toward the caravansary.

The procession swung on down the street. When the tinkle of the camel bells had ceased, Ben David re-entered his house, wondering again within him, and the wistful hopes of his fathers came to him. "Is it possible," he murmured, "that this child is really he?" And he was vexed with his own indifference and said: "I have been too careless. Tomorrow I will surely find the child." But in the morning men were waiting for him at the door to bargain. And so it always was. Day after day he said: "Tomorrow I will take the time to find the child."

But alas, the morrow never came. Days wore into

weeks, weeks into months, and months now journeyed into years. Ben David was an old man now. His hair was white and his beard was long and gray. Younger men now kept the vineyards, and he lived prosperously on the rich fruitage of his thrift.

But though prosperous he was not content. He had not entirely forgotten the child. Lately there had begun to drift into Bethlehem from the north rumors of a wondrous peasant-teacher from Nazareth of Galilee whom thousands sometimes followed; who laid his hand with healing upon the sick folk, and who spoke golden words which once heard could never be forgotten. Ben David speculated who this might be and faintly wished that he might find him.

Once more it was springtime, the fragrance of the almond blossoms was in the air. The Passover season had come, and Ben David went up with others to Jerusalem to attend the feast. Drifting idly with the crowds of pilgrims who thronged the streets in holiday attire, he found himself one day not far from that green hill outside the city wall where three grim crosses, with their weight of human woe, lifted themselves against a stormy sky. He heard the roar of people as they boiled against that cross like angry waves, and turning to a citizen of Jerusalem, he asked: "What may these things mean?"

"Hast thou not heard of the prophet of Nazareth," said the other, "whom the rulers are crucifying because he stirreth up the people?"

Ben David made no answer, but pushed his way through the crowd until he stood close to the heart of this strange tragedy. There he looked and listened and pondered. What a wondrous face was that upon the cross! Surely this man deserved better of his nation. Rumor spoke only well of him. And who was this woman kneeling there in such a broken, pitiful agony of suffering? Just then the man upon the cross spoke to the woman kneeling at his feet. He uttered the one word "Mother." At that the woman lifted her face. The full light of the stormy sky fell upon it, and in an instant Ben David knew it. The years had left their mark upon it, but it was the same expression of mingled purity and pain. It was the face of one into whose heart a sword had entered, and in Ben David's memory it looked up at him again out of the dusk of a December evening more than thirty years before. Lifting his glance for a moment to the wondrous face of the man upon the cross, Ben David realized as in a flash of light that *at last he had found the child.*

But it was too late. His long delay had lost for him the boon of the divine companion. He turned sadly away and was among those who returned to Jerusalem that day smiting upon their breasts in an agony of remorse. Tossing restlessly upon his bed that night in the caravansary at Jerusalem, he thought of many things.

Memory traveled back across the years to that December twilight when there was no room in the inn and he, sitting on the steps of his spacious house, had listened in vain to the appeal for shelter. He heard again in the silent streets of Bethlehem the hurrying steps of the shepherds. He knew then that he had been a hard, self-centered man, too much concerned with the orchards and the gardens.

Then up out of the depths of his consciousness, like and unsealed fountain, gushed strange words from the

sacred scriptures of his people—words that he thought
he had forgotten: "He was wounded for our transgres-
sions, he was bruised for our iniquities: the chastise-
ment of our peace was upon him; and with his stripes
we are healed." Somehow those words connected themselves with the face of the man upon the cross. Then
Ben David knew it was not too late. Tears of repent-
ance lay hot upon his cheeks, but hope shone through
them as stars that glint from out of a misty sky.

They will tell you in Bethlehem how Ben David
spent the last declining years of his life. He mellowed
and softened like the ripening fruit of his own
orchards. His house was full of hospitality. No traveler
sought refuge there in vain. He was as busy in doing
good as he had been in tilling his gardens. He talked
always of the child, and in the quiet evenings he
would gather the youth of Bethlehem about him in the
mouth of the cave where Christ was born. There he
would rehearse the wondrous story, dwell sadly upon
his own long delay, and urge upon them all the im-
mediacy of finding and following the child, who alone
could give them joy and peace and satisfaction.[10]

NO ROOM IN THE INN

It is today as in the old, old day—
   "No room in the inn."
And I think the Saviour is about to be born
   As he was then.
I have no walls of gilded splendor
   Or eiderdown bed,
But I have a humble little shelter
   To proffer instead.

I will sweep the cobwebs out of my heart
    With a broom of desire
And set the brightest candle burning
    And kindle a fire,
The softest bed and a pale pink cradle
    With pillows adorn,
Then opening my heart's door, "Here is a place
    For the Christ to be born."

                —RUBY DELL BAUGHER [11]

PRAYER:

O Father God, who leadest the races of men by thy marvelous hand, we thank thee that two thousand years ago thou didst send thy Son to this earth, giving a thrill of glory to this worn and weary world, and that thou didst reveal the way of salvation through love and the cross. But we have failed to understand this great mystery and are driven mad with our struggles and dissensions. From the depths of our hearts we repent, and like wise men of old, we press forward, with our eyes fixed on the radiant star! Amen. [12]

Co-operation

We are all earth's children,
Children of hunger and thirst, of tears and laughter,
Of weakness and strength, of fear and hope,
The one needing the many and the many needing the one,
And all the children of one Father.

—CLYDE MCGEE [13]

SCRIPTURE: I Corinthians 12:12-31.

HYMN: "Onward, Christian Soldiers."

THE STORIES:

One evening years ago in the province of Alberta, Canada, a young father and mother and their small boy went out for a stroll through a near-by wheat field. As they wandered through the waving grain, each thought the other held the hand of the child. Suddenly they realized that the boy was not with them. They called out, but there was no answer. Becoming more disturbed, they hunted frantically but without success. Finally the father went to the village and organized a searching party. For two days they went without sleep, and then someone suggested that all join hands surrounding the entire grain field, thus leaving not a single square foot uncovered in a last effort. Following this plan, they advanced on the field and soon came across the body of the child. A hush spread over them as they realized they were too late—the child was dead.

34

As the group stood there with bowed heads someone whispered: "If only we had joined hands before it was too late."

Once upon a time an old man called his sons around him when he was about to die. He wanted to impress upon them that union is strength, and so he showed them a number of small sticks of wood. He handed one to each son and said, "Break it." Each stick was broken easily. Then he took sticks of the same size, fastened them together in one bundle, and said to the strongest son, "Break it." The son exerted all his strength but he could not break it.

"I am going to paint the house," said a big can of paint, waiting already mixed in the woodshed.

"No, I'm going to paint it," the paintbrush asserted, bristling with impatience.

"You are, are you?" sneered the ladder, leaning against the wall.

"How far will either of you go without me to pay the bill?" said the checkbook of the owner of the house, in a voice muffled from the pocket of the coat hanging on a nail.

Just then the painter, who had overheard these remarks, ventured to put in a word: "Perhaps I'd better take a holiday," he said quietly, "I wonder if the house will be painted by the time I return?"

Even the most efficient of us is only a tool in the hands of an infinite world.

PRAYER:

O God, we thank thee for the growing sense of oneness in aspirations, purposes, and goals which bind together our common humanity. Wilt thou help us that the spirit of co-operation and service be ingrained in our lives so that all may have opportunity to live abundantly. May the spirit of tolerance, good will, and sacrificial service grow in our hearts and in the lives of people everywhere so that we may work together as a world family. We know that we are praying in thy name. Amen.

Everyday Christianity

To seek for the reproduction of Christ's mind in the mind of the community is the greatest aim that we can cherish.

—PHILLIPS BROOKS

SCRIPTURE: Ephesians 6:13-18.

HYMNS: "I Want a Principle Within"; "Guide Me, O Thou Great Jehovah."

THE STORY:

A man had occasion to go to a certain town for the first time. He arrived on a blustery December day. As he moved along the street he saw people in fur coats strangely walking in bare feet. They all seemed prosperous, but no one wore shoes, and many limped along suffering with chilblains and bruises. Arriving at the hotel he found the bellboys barefooted.

At luncheon he sat with a prosperous old gentleman who wore no shoes. As this new acquaintance seemed kindly disposed the traveler asked: "Pardon me if I seem intrusive, but I perceive that no one in this town wears shoes. Would you mind telling me why?"

"Ah," said the old gentleman piously, "why indeed?" He admitted that shoes were desirable and that everybody should wear them but he could not tell why they did not do so.

The traveler took a walk around the town and saw

37

here and there buildings more beautiful and larger than ordinary. Seeing the janitor sweeping at the doorway of one of them he stopped.

"What is this building? I am a stranger and notice that there are several similar buildings in this town."

"This is a shoe factory," replied the janitor.

"So they make shoes here?" was the question.

"Oh, not at all," replied the man, "they just talk about making shoes, and sing about making shoes, and pray about making shoes. They never make them here."

The janitor said that once every seven days all other businesses closed and people came to hear about shoes. But no shoes were produced and no one wore them.

Our friend moved on and finally in a little side street he actually found an old cobbler making shoes.

"Do these people wear shoes sometimes?" he asked.

"I make a pair for nearly every bride and groom," said the old cobbler. "They wear them on the day of the ceremony and when the babies are christened. That day even the baby himself wears bootees. But they would be conspicuous if they wore them at any other time, so they take them off immediately after the ceremony. The bootees are quickly removed too, for they do not want the child cramped in any way. They say they will wait until the child gets old enough to decide for himself and then if he wants shoes he shall have them," he explained.

"Aren't the shoes ever worn again?" asked the traveler.

"Yes, when they die we always put shoes on the feet of folks. Then even those who have never worn shoes and who have hated them are given a pair."

The traveler then bought a pair of fine shoes for

the kindly old gentleman with whom he had eaten lunch, as the old man had winced at every step he took and seemed to suffer so without them.

Strange as it may seem, however, the traveler was thanked for his kindness, but the old man did not feel he could wear them.

"The better people are not doing it," he said, "and I would be considered fanatical." [14]

We do not lay hold on the Christian life to wear it every day, but lay it aside for special occasions. Yet it is the only force which will bear us up, protect, and sustain.

FEET

> Where the sun shines in the street
> There are very many feet
> Seeking God, all unaware
> That their hastening is a prayer.
> Perhaps these feet would deem it odd
> (Who think they are on business bent)
> If someone went,
> And told them, "You are seeking God."
> —MARY CAROLINE DAVIES

PRAYER:

> I would, dear Jesus, I could break
> The hedge that creeds and hearsay make,
> And, like the first disciples, be
> In person led and taught by thee
>
> I read thy words, so strong and sweet;
> I seek the footprints of thy feet;
> But men so mystify the trace,
> I long to see thee face to face. Amen.
> —JOHN D. LONG

The Face Mirrors Character

To change and change is life; to move and never rest;
Not what we are, but what we hope is best.
—JAMES RUSSELL LOWELL

SCRIPTURE: Philippians 4:8-9.

HYMNS: "Dear Lord and Father of Mankind"; "Jesus,
Lover of My Soul."

THE STORY:

A king with supreme power over many people had
ruled wisely but with sternness. He seldom smiled.

But one day he fell in love with a beautiful young
princess. She was not only lovely in face and figure
but was of a gentle and kindly nature. The king looked
into his mirror and feared that the young maiden
would be frightened at his stern visage, which did not
even lighten when he strove to smile.

He went to a magician. "Make me a mask, thin and
delicate, painting upon it the features of a handsome
and kindly face," he requested.

"That is not easily done," replied the old man, "for
your own face must conform to that of the mask. If,
after putting it on, you once frown or the stern lines
deepen around your mouth, the mask will break."

"I will do my part to make your work a success,"
promised the king.

And so a handsome mask was made for him. It was

so delicately wrought that it conformed to his features but rendered them gracious and kindly.

"Remember you will have to live the character of your mask," warned the old magician.

"I'll remember," promised the king.

The ruler then sued for the princess' hand in marriage and in time she accepted him. The king's change in nature surprised the court, but they attributed it to the influence of his sweet young wife.

There were times when he had difficulty in living up to his new face, but because of his self-control the mask remained unimpaired. He would not disappoint his beloved, and he became so kindly, so generous, and so truehearted that the fact that he was wearing a mask bothered him. He realized that he had tricked his lovely queen. One day he went to the magician again and requested: "Take off this deceiving mask. I cannot wear it longer."

"Remember," counseled the magician, "I cannot make another. You will have to show your own face if I destroy this mask."

"Very well," agreed the king, "I cannot continue to deceive my wife."

The magician removed the mask and strange to say the appearance of the king was not altered. His kindly deeds and generous thoughts had caused his face to look like the mask.

APPROACHES

When thou turnest away from ill,
Christ is this side of thy hill.

When thou turnest toward good,
Christ is walking in thy wood.

When thy heart says, "Father, pardon!"
Then the Lord is in thy garden.

When stern duty wakes to watch,
Then His hand is on the latch.

But when hope thy song doth rouse,
Then the Lord is in thy house.

When to love is all thy wit,
Christ doth at thy table sit.

When God's will is thy heart's pole,
Then Christ is thy very soul.
                              —GEORGE MacDONALD

PRAYER:

O Lord, our Christ, may we have thy mind and thy
spirit; make us instruments of thy peace; where there
is hatred, let us sow love; where there is injury, pardon;
where there is discord, union; where there is doubt,
faith; where there is despair, hope; where there is darkness, light; and where there is sadness, joy. O divine
Master, grant that we may not so much seek to be
consoled as to console; to be understood, as to understand; to be loved, as to love; for it is in giving that we
receive, it is in pardoning that we are pardoned, and
it is in dying that we are born to eternal life. Amen.[15]

Faith

Faith is the flickering candle
Lighting the mind's dim room,
Piercing with its rays of hope
The outer gloom.

—Marion Lee [16]

Scripture: Hebrews 11:1-3; 12:1-2.

Hymns: "My Faith Looks Up to Thee"; "Blessed Assurance."

The Story:

It was a hot summer and there had been no rain for a long time. The beautiful lawns around the comfortable houses in the village were dry and parched, and the leaves were dropping from the trees. The people dared not spare water for their most cherished flowers as the wells were almost dry. There was even danger that the drinking water might become impure.

The farmers were desperate. Their stock needed water and their fields were blistering in the sun. Finally a committee called upon the minister and requested that he conduct a special prayer service for rain. The time was set for noon the next day.

Before noon next day all the people in the town and surrounding country left their work. They dressed in their best clothes and came to the church. The minister prayed long and feverently for rain. The members

43

each prayed that showers might be sent to their parched land. While they prayed a cloud formed, the sky darkened, and great drops of water began to fall. They could hardly believe their eyes. Shaking each other by the hand, laughing and crying together, they watched the miracle of the rain.

But the rain did not stop. It continued to pour down throughout the afternoon. At last it became necessary for them to go home. Looking ruefully at the water-soaked, dripping landscape, and then at their Sunday clothes, they suddenly realized that no one had brought an umbrella. They had prayed for rain but no one had had the faith that God would answer their prayers.

From THE HIGHER CATECHISM

And what is faith? The anchored trust that at the core of
    things
Health, goodness, animating strength flow from exhaust-
    less springs;
That no star rolls unguided down the rings of endless
    maze,
That no feet tread an aimless path through wastes of
    empty days;
That trusts the everlasting voice, the glad, calm voice that
    saith
That order grows from chaos, and that life is born from
    death;
That from the wreck of rending stars behind the storm
    and scathe,
There dwells a heart of central calm—and this, and this
    is faith.

—SAM WALTER FOSS [17]

Prayer:

Almighty and merciful Father, whose power and whose love work together for the good of thy children, we pray:

for faith to believe that thou dost rule the world;

for faith to believe that if we seek first the kingdom and righteousness thou wilt provide for all our lesser needs;

for faith to keep calm and brave in face of danger;

for faith to put our trust in love rather than in force;

for faith to leave in thy hands the welfare of our dear ones;

for faith to rid ourselves of all vain anxieties and paralyzing fears, that our best strength may be devoted to thy service.

In Christ's name. Amen.

Forgiveness

Truants from love, we dream of wrath,
  O rather let us trust the more!
Through all the wanderings of the path,
  We still can see our father's door.
            —OLIVER WENDELL HOLMES

SCRIPTURE: I John 1:5-10; Luke 11:2-4; John 20:21-23.

HYMNS: "Amazing Grace"; "There's a Wideness in God's Mercy."

THE STORY:

The train was moving swiftly along, and as Mr. Brown sat quietly reading he felt the restlessness of the young man across the aisle. After sitting with his head in his hands awhile, he would fidget from side to side in his seat. Then he would pace up and down the aisle. Mr. Brown felt that there was definitely something wrong with the boy. At last the older man arose and crossing the aisle he asked: "Son, can I help you? You look worried."

The young man was startled: "I hardly know how you can help me, sir," he answered, "but I'll tell you my story. About four years ago I had a disagreement with my father. He told me to get out and said that he never wanted to see me again. My mother pleaded with us but we were both stubborn and I left home.

46

I have not heard from them for four years. I went west and got a good job, working steadily. But all the time I have longed to see my home folks.

"I decided to come back at last and so I wrote a letter to my mother, telling them I was sorry I had caused them grief. I wrote that I would like to see them and would pass through my home town on a certain date. If father was willing that I come home, I asked her to hang a white rag on the willow tree facing the railroad track. If I saw it, I would get off the train and come home. Now, Mister, we are getting near my town. My parents' home is on the edge of town just as we reach the river. It is a little white cottage on the left side and stands alone—you can't miss it. I don't dare to look—will you tell me if she has tied a white rag on the willow tree?"

"Indeed I will, son," reassured Mr. Brown.

So the boy sat with his head in his hands, tensely waiting while the train pulled into town. Mr. Brown looking intently out of the window, observing every house until unmistakably the white house came into view. There it was near the river with a large willow tree facing the railroad. His eyes grew misty as he saw a white rag on every branch of the willow tree. Not content with this the mother had also adorned every bush and tree in the yard with the welcome pennant.

"Son," shouted Mr. Brown, "get ready to go home, your parents are waiting."

THE TRUE NEED

I do not wish to see my sins more plain,
But this: to know Thy life, without a stain.

I would not see the vileness of my heart,
But this would know: how pure and true Thou art.

I would forget my paltry life, so small,
And know Thy greatness, Thou, my All in All.

Oh, teach me not how deep my spirit's night,
But flood me with Thy beams, Thou Perfect Light!
—THOMAS CURTIS CLARK [18]

PRAYER:

Our loving Father, we remember the ancient promise
that if we confess our sins thou art faithful and just
to forgive us our sins, and to cleanse us from all un-
righteousness. We thank thee for thy grace and mercy
in the past and we ask thee, because of our great
need to do that which we cannot do alone, to make
us strong where we are weak and to help us stand
against all evils of our time. Forgive our failures to
understand thy will for us, and lead us into the Kingdom of God, which is righteousness and peace and
joy. Through Jesus Christ our Lord, Amen.

Giving

Give! as the morning that flows out of heaven;
Give! as the waves when their channel is riven;
Give! as the free air and sunshine are given;
    Lavishly, utterly, joyfully give!
Not the waste drops of thy cup overflowing;
Not the faint sparks of thy hearth ever glowing;
Not a pale bud from the June roses blowing;
    Give as He gave thee who gave thee to live.
—ROSE TERRY COOKE

SCRIPTURE: Malachi 3:7-10; Micah 7:7-9.

HYMNS: "I Love Thy Kingdom, Lord"; "We Give
Thee but Thine Own."

THE STORY:

A man went shopping. He bought himself a new
suit for fifty dollars, a new hat for ten dollars, a pair
of shoes for ten dollars, and a good-looking shirt and
a handsome tie to go with it for five dollars. After
this he felt pretty good. Carrying all his purchases,
he was making his way toward his car and home when
suddenly he thought "If I go home with these new
clothes, I must take something to my wife."

So he stopped at the first woman's shop that he
passed and asked for a dress for his wife. As he stood
near a rack of house dresses the saleswoman showed
him one for three dollars. It looked about the right
size, so she wrapped it up for him.

49

Bursting into the door of his home, he cried out: "Here I am, dear! See what I have brought you! It expresses my love and devotion! Whatever I spend for you, is really yours all the time. Here is the gift."

The wife opened the package containing the poorly fitting dress, and then she looked at the heap of packages on the hall table.

"And those?" she asked.

"Oh, these I bought for myself," he said proudly.

He opened them up displaying the handsome suit, the becoming hat, the shiny shoes, the well-cut shirt, and the dashing tie.

Think you he fooled his wife?

Neither do we fool God.

IT IS MORE BLESSED

Pour out thy love like the rush of a river,
Wasting its waters, forever and ever,
Through the burnt sands that reward not the giver;
　　Silent or songful, thou nearest the sea.
Scatter thy life as the summer's shower pouring;
What if no bird through the pearl rain is soaring?
What if no blossom looks upward adoring?
　　Look to the life that was lavished for thee!

So the wild wind strews its perfumed caresses;
Evil and thankless the desert it blesses;
Bitter the wave that its soft pinion presses;
　　Never it ceaseth to whisper and sing.
What if the hard heart gives thorns for thy roses?
What if on rocks thy tired bosom reposes?
Sweeter is music with minor-keyed closes,
　　Fairest the vines that on ruin will cling.

Almost the day of thy giving is over;
Ere from the grass dies the bee-haunted clover
Thou wilt have vanished from friend and from lover;
    What shall thy longing avail in the grave?
Give as the heart gives whose fetters are breaking,
Live, love, and hope, all thy dreams and thy waking;
Soon heaven's river thy soul-fever slaking,
    Thou shalt know God and the gift that he gave.

               —Rose Terry Cooke

PRAYER:

Our Father, who makest all things new, we would share with thee thy purpose for the world. We pray that something like thy love and concern may grow in our hearts. For what thy church is able to do in behalf of a more kind and just world, we are grateful. Reveal to us more clearly thy purpose and inspire us to labor and give more freely of the blessings which thou hast given us. May we be drawn into fellowship with all peoples of the earth, and belong truly to the church of the living God. Amen.

Growth

There is no standing still! Even as I pause
The steep path shifts and I slip back apace,
No idling on the pathway hard and slow,
I must go forward or must backward go.
—Author Unknown

Scripture: Psalm 92:12-15; Matthew 6:28-30.

Hymns: "Take Time to Be Holy"; "Holy Spirit, Faithful Guide."

The Story:

Close to the shore of a beautiful lake, far back in the mountains, grew a very tall pine tree. Its branches reached out and out, trying to drink in more and more of the clear air and bright sunshine; its roots reached far down into the earth, trying to gather more and more nourishment from the soil; its top reached up and tried to see what was above the fleecy white cloud floating over it; its trunk was straight and strong as it had need to be when the cold northwest winds of winter blew over the lake.

One day the old pine felt someone digging near its roots and looking down it saw a little spruce tree being planted there. Then it rustled all its branches and needles for very joy. Here would be someone to talk to and someone to help to grow.

52

After the roots of the spruce tree were fairly well set, it began looking around to see who its new neighbors might be, and close beside it found the trunk of the pine tree. The spruce followed it up and up until it was almost dizzy.

"Oh," it said, "what a big, big tree! How glad I am to be planted close beside it. Perhaps some day I can grow to be just like it."

That night when all was still, the little tree heard a whisper, so it listened, for it felt that it came from the pine tree. Then it heard the old pine say: "Little Spruce tree, I'm so glad you have come to live near me. Can I help you in any way?"

"Yes, indeed you can," said the little tree. "I have been looking at you all day. What a wonderful tree you are! Tell me how to grow to be as tall and straight as you are."

"That is not a hard thing to tell, but it is a very hard thing to do," said the old pine. "Keep looking up every day and let nothing bend or break you. You must desire with all your might to be one of the best trees, and then grow and grow."

"That I will do and I will keep close by you so that I may grow like you," answered the spruce tree happily.

The days passed by and every night the little spruce looked carefully to see if its trunk was just as straight as the trunk of the old pine tree. And because it had such a splendid tree to copy, it too grew straight and strong. When the winter came the cold winds whistled about the little tree, but the old pine was a little in front of the spruce and saved it from some of the force of the wind. At night when all was still again the pine would whisper: "That was a hard breeze, little one, but it is over and you have gained strength by fighting it. Now look up, and straighten up, so that all the bend may be taken out of you. Measure your trunk by mine if you like." And the little tree would murmur its thanks, straighten its trunk, and nestle close to its big, strong friend.

Finally after many years the little tree had grown so tall that its top just reached the lowest branches of the pine. How proud it was! "Oh," it said, "I have looked up at you so long, and now at last I can really touch you. I'm so happy I don't care whether I grow any more or not."

But the old pine answered thoughtfully: "Oh, you mustn't think of stopping growing now. Why, the world gets bigger and lovelier the higher up I grow. There's much more to see, and it's much easier to breathe up here. Come up, child, come up."

So the little spruce pushed ahead until its branches were mingled with the middle branches of the pine. How happy they were talking together! How many beautiful things they saw around the mountain lake. Then the spruce found, to its surprise, that the old pine was still growing, still pushing up, still making sure it did not bend.

"Aren't you ready to stop soon?" asked the spruce. "Surely you are big enough now."

But the old pine answered: "I shall never be big enough. I want always to grow. I have heard that there are trees in my family that have grown to be many times as big as I, and I want to be one of the best." So the spruce spread its roots wide and deep, sent its branches far out for light and air, and kept growing toward the sky. "Always," it said, "I too will keep looking up. I will let nothing bend or break me, I will desire with all my heart to be the best possible tree and grow and grow."[19]

GROWING

"Mother, do you still grow?"

I let the measuring rod
Slip closer to my child's head—
Three foot two!—
"Do I still grow?"
Do I still grow?

This afternoon I suffered
From unkind words
But smiled.
Last year I would have been
Quite proud
Of making sharp retort.

Last week I set aside
My own desires
For others.

Last year I would have cried,
"I'll have my way
Let others yield to me."

Last month I found some beauty
In a soul once scorned,
And told it to another.

Do I still grow?
Yes, child,
But oh! so slowly!
—MARY DICKERSON BANGHAM [20]

PRAYER:

Dear Lord, teach us to become little children once more, to stand wide-eyed before the mystery around us, and to realize that what we know is but a trifle in the light of thine infinite wisdom. Help us to grow in grace and knowledge, and to so number our days that courage, faith, hope, and love may live and abide in us. May we "grow in grace, and in the knowledge of our Lord and Saviour Jesus Christ." Amen.

Guiding a Child

I took a piece of plastic clay
And idly fashioned it one day,
And as my fingers pressed it still,
It moved and yielded to my will.

I came again when days were past—
The bit of clay was hard at last;
The form I gave it, it still bore,
But I could change that form no more.

I took a piece of living clay
And gently formed it day by day,
And moulded with my power and art
A young child's soft and yielding heart.

I came again when years were gone—
It was a man I looked upon;
He still that early impress wore,
And I could change him nevermore.

—AUTHOR UNKNOWN

SCRIPTURE: Proverbs 31:25-29.

HYMNS: "O Happy Home"; "Shepherd of Tender Youth."

THE STORY:

A blind woman had a son who was the joy of her life. Though she had no sight of her eyes, yet she was skillful of her hands, and it was her delight to

57

make pretty clothes for her boy, soft and fine and full of delicate stitches.

One day the boy came to her and said: "Mother, give me some other clothes to wear. These are too small and tight for me. Moreover, they are baby clothes and my playfellows mock and laugh at me because of them."

But the mother said: "Nay, my darling, these are by far the best clothes for you. Let mother make them for you always. See how soft and warm they are, and pretty too, I know, although I cannot see them. Be content, for you are my own darling son and so you must remain."

When the boy found that he could not persuade her, he held his peace, and he withdrew from his playmates.

Then he went out and looked about him and found the hide of a wolf and the pelt of a fox and huddled them around him over his baby frock, and so went among his mates. Only when he came back to the room where his mother sat, he threw aside the skins and came to her in his frock; and she kissed him and felt the frills and the silken stitches, and said rejoicing: "You are my own darling little son."

By and by there was a war in that country and all the young men went out to meet the enemy. Some were clad in armor, others in leather jackets and doublets, and with them went the son of the blind woman in his frock.

Then when the woman knew that her son was gone, she wept and lamented and ran out into the street. There she met one who was returning from the field of battle, and she asked him how went the fight. "Bravely," he replied, "our men did well, all save one, who had no weapon and whom I saw beaten down."

"Oh, stranger," cried the blind woman, "was that one a little boy—a sweet child with pretty clothes all wrought with needlework?"

"Nay," said the stranger, "it was a man, half-naked, huddled in the skins of beasts, with strange rags showing under the skins."

"Oh," said the woman, "I wonder who that poor soul might be, and I wonder when my darling son will come home to me again."

And even while she spoke her son lay dead, and huddled around him was the hide of a wolf and the pelt of a fox, with baby clothes fluttering from under them.[21]

A CHILD WENT FORTH

There was a child went forth every day,
And the first object he look'd upon, that object he became,
And that object became part of him for the day or a certain part of the day,
Or for many years or stretching cycles of years.

The early lilacs became part of this child,

.   .   .   .

And the apple trees cover'd with blossoms and the fruit afterward, and wood-berries, and the commonest weeds by the road,

.   .   .   .

The blow, the quick loud word, the tight bargain, the crafty lure,
The family usages, the language, the company, the furniture, the yearning and swelling heart,

.   .   .   .

These became part of that child who went forth every
day, and who now goes, and will always go forth everyday.

—WALT WHITMAN

PRAYER:

Our Father, God, we ask thy blessing on all those
who guide and teach the children of the world. As
they are taught, so shall the nations of the future
be. Teach us to reverence young life and reward us
with a sense of our own part in thy great plan for
thy children. Amen.

Handicaps

For insights won through toil and tears,
We thank Thee, Keeper of our years.
                              —CLYDE McGEE [22]

SCRIPTURE: Psalm 67.

HYMNS: "Blessed Assurance"; "Pass Me Not, O Gentle
    Saviour."

THE STORY:

Some of the hymns we sing so easily, and that
give us a lift toward God, were written by Fanny Jane
Crosby, who became blind when a few weeks old.
Fanny Crosby was born March 24, 1820, in Putnam
County, New York, of Christian parents. She owed
much to her grandmother who interpreted life to her
and who gave her word pictures of the lovely things
of nature and God. She learned to ride horseback and
to climb fences and had a healthy, happy childhood in
spite of her handicap. Very early she wrote rhymes
and loved poetry. When only eight years old she wrote
these lines:

> O what a happy girl am I!
>   Although I cannot see,
> I am resolved that in this world
>   Contented I will be.
>
> How many blessings I enjoy
>   That other people don't.

To weep and sigh because I'm blind
I cannot and I won't.

She learned the lines written by Milton on his blindness, and when she was a child she could repeat many passages from Psalms, Proverbs, and the book of Ruth, and much of the New Testament. All her life she prized the memory treasures her grandmother helped her to store away.

But she did want to learn to read, and finally the way was opened for her to go to the New York Institution for the Blind. She studied there for over twelve years and then remained as a teacher for eleven years longer. She was a great favorite and was able to help the pupils because she understood so well their problems.

Her love for sacred music began when as a child she imagined the birds singing to their Creator. She felt that she too would like to thank God and to talk to him in beautiful words. She began to write poems which were set to music. Her hymns were translated into other languages and sung around the world.

A little blind girl in Korea was called "Fanny Crosby" because her voice was sweet and she sang the Crosby hymns as if inspired. People came for miles around to hear her sing.

"Pass Me Not, O Gentle Saviour" was Miss Crosby's first hymn to win world-wide favor. "Blessed Assurance," "Safe in the Arms of Jesus," and "Saved by Grace" are among the most famous of her hymns. She lived to be ninety-four years old, and died in 1915 having written over six thousand hymns and having brought a blessing to the lives of countless people.

A PRAYER FOR INSPIRATION

The prayers I make will then be sweet indeed,
  If thou the spirit give by which I pray:
  My unassisted heart is barren clay,
Which of its native self can nothing feed;
Of good and pious works Thou art the seed
  Which quickens where Thou say'st it may;
  Unless Thou show us then Thine own true way,
No man can find it! Father, Thou must lead!
Do Thou, then, breathe those thoughts into my mind
  By which such virtue may in me be bred
  That in Thy holy footsteps I may tread;
The fetters of my tongue do Thou unbind,
  That I may have the power to sing of Thee,
  And sound Thy praises everlastingly.

—MICHELANGELO
(Trans. William Wordsworth)

PRAYER:

Father in heaven, for all who watch and wait and weep; for all who have lost heart, and are fearful of the footfall of despair; for those who feel that nothing matters now, and have relaxed their watch where unrelenting temptation hides in the shadows; for eyes which have grown weary scanning a sailless sea for ships which have never come in; for those whose love has gone unrequited and whose hungry hearts are starved; for those who have lost the faith which once was theirs, and voyage strange and stormy seas alone— for all these we pray that of thy mercy thou wouldst restore their unshepherded souls, and lead them in right paths for thy name's sake. Amen.

—HUBERT L. SIMPSON

The Importance of the Child

The best investment is in children. You had better take a good look at them as they pass you on the street, for they are the ones who are going to make a new world for you, and you can catch some glimmer of the dawn in their faces.

—WILLIAM CAMERON

SCRIPTURE: Matthew 19:13-15; 18:1-6.

HYMN: "I Think when I Read that Sweet Story of Old."

THE CHILD'S APPEAL

I am the Child.
All the world waits for my coming.
All the earth watches with interest to see what I shall become.
Civilization hangs in the balance,
For what I am, the world of tomorrow will be.

I am the Child.
I have come into your world, about which I know nothing.
Why I came I know not;
How I came I know not;
I am curious; I am interested.

I am the Child.
You hold in your hand my destiny.
You determine, largely, whether I shall succeed or fail.
Give me, I pray you, those things that make for happiness.

Train me, I beg you, that I may be a blessing to the world.

—MAMIE GENE COLE

THE STORY:

There was once a woman who had a beautiful garden. It was landscaped so that each flower in its place seemed perfect. The earliest spring blossoms were masses of fragrant loveliness, and before they were gone the later spring flowers were beginning to bloom.

Every evening she walked there, rejoicing as she saw big strong plants, well pruned, watered, and cared for. She had an excellent gardener.

One evening as she walked she peered over the hedge and saw a very unattractive spot—small plants just coming up, others not yet blooming, and then rows upon rows of clay pots with just a sprig of green showing.

"How ugly!" she cried. "And so close to my beautiful garden."

The next morning she called her caretaker. "I do not want you to trouble with seedlings and small plants," she said. "Turn the space you use for that into another garden even lovelier than this one."

"But madam," he protested, "I know the plant nursery is not sightly, unless you enjoy watching small things grow, but from where will your garden of the future come?"

"There will be time to think about that later," she ordered.

And so the gardener gave the small plants away, reserving only the largest ones to use in the new garden. The woman rejoiced and her friends exclaimed over the orderliness and the beauty of her estate.

Autumn came and winter. As the woman looked out on the snow-laden shrubs she sighed for summer and her garden. But in the spring, after the first flowering bulbs had wasted away, there were few blooms to take their place. Again she called her gardener.

"What has happened?" she cried. "Where are the flowers?"

"I am sorry, madam," he replied, "but to have a beautiful garden there must be a plant nursery for seedlings. As the older plants mature, others must be put in their places. You will not allow me to have a nursery in which to grow them, and so I have no new plants to replace those which have died in the winter."

"How foolish I was!" sighed the woman. "I begrudged the space for the small growing plants and seedlings which would have insured my garden of the future."

PRAYER:

Father of all, we thank thee for the dear ones who shelter us and whom we shelter. We are grateful for those who love us and whom, with answering love, we love back again; those under sight of our eyes and those far away. We thank thee for the tender ties that join us in one great family of love. Wilt thou help us to be patient and understanding with childhood and youth, so that they may have a place of happiness and service in our homes and churches and communities. Amen.

In Thine Own Hand

> Seek not afar for beauty. Lo! it glows
>   In dew wet grasses, all about thy feet;
>
> .   .   .   .
>
> Go not abroad for happiness. For see,
>   It is a flower that blossoms at thy door!
>
> —Minot J. Savage [25]

Scripture: Psalm 92:1-5.

Hymns: "Holy Spirit, Faithful Guide"; "He Leadeth Me."

The Story:

The factory community in Yorkshire housed many a family. For years the sons and daughters had followed in the steps of their fathers and mothers in daily toil at the looms. Music-loving they were, and many a hymn was sung to the glory and praise of God.

However, there was little of beauty around them and the people lived lives of hard work and little pleasure. But always in the homes love blossomed and families were bound together with concern for each other. Musical instruments were few and the old fiddle in Charles's home was the plaything of all the children. Charles himself had picked out a hymn or two by twanging the strings with his fingers. His father had been known to draw an old bow across it and

67

get music, but it was remembered that his grandfather had loved to play upon the instrument, and with it could draw tears or bring a lilt of happiness to the heart.

Charles, being the oldest of the family, went to work very young, and after a few years, when his brothers and sisters grew up, the house seemed to him too small and the village too limited. He told his father he must go away—he must find beauty and he must find treasure. His father looked at him questionly, and then said slowly: "Son, you are free to go but always remember that love and concern for others must go with pleasure and beauty, or life is tasteless."

What strange advice, thought the boy, as he left his home, not once looking back.

The world was gay, he found, when he had money, but the little money an untrained worker could earn soon disappeared, and with it his friends. He wandered from place to place and was often lonely. One thing alone gave him pleasure—music. He would sit in the poorest gallery seat to listen to great musicians, and once he bought a cheap violin that he himself might express the harmonies that were within him.

Finally he found himself in Italy playing on street corners. Many paused to hear him, and finally an old man stopped to speak to him kindly. "Son," he said, "I like your music. I too am a musician. Will you come home with me for a bite to eat?"

Gladly the boy accompanied him to his modest home, and that day a friendship was formed and for some time the music master patiently taught Charles in his moments of leisure. The boy felt that he had found beauty. The years passed and with them the old music master. Charles was often lonely and treasure eluded him. He found himself wandering again from city to city, playing his violin on the corners of the streets. Love and friendship passed him by.

At last he decided to return to Yorkshire for a visit. He forgot the ugliness of his home town, the narrowness of the villagers, and remembered with longing the kindliness and love of his family and friends. On his arrival everything looked familiar, but he discovered that his mother had died and that one of his brothers lived in the family home, the father then being an old man.

"And what have you found out in the world, my boy?" asked the patriarch.

"I have found beauty through music, but I have little of treasure," sighed the son.

"Treasure enough, my boy, but play for me your music," invited the father.

"The way was long and I did not bring my violin," said Charles. The old man reached up high to a rafter and brought down the old fiddle, its strings intact.

"Remember this one?" he smiled.

The son tuned it and started to play. The little room had never heard such heavenly harmony as poured forth, and the son himself seemed transported to another realm as he played. Finally he stopped.

The father with tears in his eyes embraced him. "It is yours!" he cried. "The fiddle is yours. No one else shall ever play it."

And then as the son wonderingly caressed the violin he peered inside and saw the name of the world's most famous violin maker—Antonius Stradivarius, Cremona, 1690.

The treasure was his, and had been in his home all the time.

PRAYER FOR A LITTLE HOME

God send us a little home
To come back to when we roam—
Low walls and fluted tiles;
Wide windows, a view for miles;
Red firelight and deep chairs;
Small white beds upstairs;
Great talk in little nooks;
Dim colors, rows of books;
One picture on each wall;
Not many things at all.
God send us a little ground—
Tall trees standing round,
Homely flowers in brown sod,
Overhead Thy stars, O God!
God bless when winds blow
Our home and all we know.

—FLORENCE BONE

PRAYER:

Eternal God, we confess we are slow to understand what thy Kingdom is. Bring to our remembrance the Master's own word that the Kingdom of God is within us. Thy self-sacrificing love is loose in the world, seeking to redeem us. Give us a vision of the world for which Christ died, and help us to dedicate ourselves to its realization wherever we are, whatever we do, whatever we say. In the name of Christ. Amen.

The Loom of Life

A tapestry of promise is weaving in my loom,
The Creator of the pattern today is making room
For bright and radiant colors of promises divine—
He bids me take the blessed threads and make them truly
    mine;
"As thy days thy strength shall be," this thread of gold
    so strong
Is weaving with the silver "He is my strength, my song";
A strand of royal purple brings "All sufficient grace."
Lo! Many threads are weaving now, in pattern finding
    place.
    Dear Lord, guide well my shuttle,
    May all my weaving be
    True to the perfect pattern—
    My promised tapestry.

—Adah Lyle Kidder [24]

SCRIPTURE: Job 7:6-10.

HYMNS: "I Need Thee Every Hour"; "Thou My Everlasting Portion."

THE STORY:

The sun had set and the shadows were deepening in the valleys. The cry of a night bird came from a clump of pines on the mountainside. In the faint flush of the western sky hung the crescent moon, pale and silvery. Up the narrow, winding path that led to the home of the Master Weaver, two maidens were toiling. One was tall and beautiful, gray-eyed and golden-haired; the other small and dark-haired and gentle faced. Coming at length to the little wicket gate, they passed in between rows of old-fashioned flowers. They knocked at the door of the quaint rambling cottage. In answer to their summons there appeared in the doorway an old man with long white hair and a flowing beard. In his hand he carried a lighted candle.

"Peace be unto thee, daughters," he said in greeting. "Enter and make known thine errand."

"We have come, O Master Weaver," said the maidens, "to ask of thee thread to weave for ourselves garments of life, that we may be ready to appear before the king when he shall send for us. Canst thou meet our need?"

"Enter and thou mayest have choice," said he, leading the way into a long low room whose walls were hung from ceiling to floor with threads of every conceivable color and texture.

With a cry of delight the fair-haired maiden began choosing. Flitting about here and there, she filled her arms with soft, silken threads in shades as delicate as the tints of the rainbow. The dark-haired one hesitated a moment; then, placing her hand on the old man's arm she said gently: "Thou art so wise, O Master Weaver, the long years of thy life have been spent in this service. Thou knowest what I have need of. Wilt thou choose for me?"

There came into the face of the Master Weaver the shadow of a wonderful smile. Without answering, he turned and began gathering. A strange choice it seemed, for among the threads which he placed in her arms were few silken ones, few bright ones, and many dark and coarse.

"When thy work is finished," said he to them in parting, "come again to me that I may see if it be perfect. Thou canst not enter into the kingdom with faulty garments."

As each one's threads, so was her life. Living was weaving. Into the life of the beautiful one came days replete with pleasure. All the ease that wealth could give was hers. No thought of the need and suffering of others came to her. The beggar asking alms passed her door; the cry of the orphan went unheard; the prisoner languished in his cell. As the days and weeks lengthened into years her garment of life neared completion. Into the life of the dark-haired maiden came days of joy and gladness, days of toil and pain. Because sorrow had touched her own heart, she saw the need and sufferings in the lives of those about her. The beggar was fed from her table; the orphan clothed from her store; and the sick were soothed by the touch of her hand at the midnight hour. The prisoner in his cell listened for her footstep and the sound of her voice; the erring one turned from his way because of her gentle pleading. As the years passed her garment of life neared completion.

The sun had long set. The shadows in the valley had crept to the mountaintop and it was night. Two gray-haired women knocked at the door of the rambling cottage on the mountainside. An old man with white hair and flowing beard, bearing a lighted candle in one hand, came to meet them.

"Welcome, daughters, peace be unto thee," said he. "Wilt thou enter and tell thine errand?"

"Our work is finished, Master," said they. "Many years have we toiled. Wilt thou see if our garments are fit for the kingdom?"

She whose hair in the long ago had been gold-colored, placed her work in the hands of the Master Weaver. It was poor indeed and full of flaws. The delicate rainbow shades had faded, and the silken threads were frayed and knotted. The old man looked at it long and carefully, then handed it to her sorrowfully "Thou hast failed, my daughter," said he. "Thou canst not wear this into the presence of thy king." And with bowed head the gray-haired woman passed out into the night. Taking the garment from her whose hair in the long ago had been dark and whose face was still gentle, he held it up. It was of rare beauty. The bright silken threads were woven in among the dark heavy ones in marvelous design. "Well done, thou faithful one," said the old man, placing the garment about her shoulders. "Thou are fit indeed for the kingdom." And as he spoke a radiant light filled the little cottage room, and there came the sound of a distant sweet voice saying: "Enter thou into the joy of thy Lord." And the woman passed out and up beyond the stars into the Kingdom of God.[25]

MY TAPESTRY

I wonder how the other side will be
When I have finished weaving all my thread.
I cannot see the pattern nor the end
Of this great piece of work which is for me;
I only know that I must weave with care
The colors which are given me day by day,
And make of them a fabric firm and true

Which will do service for my fellow men.
Sometimes these colors are so dark and gray,
I doubt if there be any line or trace
Of beauty there, but all at once there comes
A thread of gold, or fair bright hue, or rose,
As deep as that at sunset after rain,
And then I know that there will always be
That one bright spot to cherish, yes, to keep,
And maybe, 'gainst its ground of darker hue
It will be beautiful.
The warp is held in place by Master hands;
The Master mind made the design for me;
If I but weave the shuttle to and fro
And blend the colors just the way I may,
Perhaps, when it is finished, he will say:
"Tis good," and place it on the footstool at His feet.
                                        —MARY MILES COLVIN

PRAYER:

Creator of all mankind, take our hands in thine
and direct all our ways that we may work in quietness
and strength. As we weave into our lives the joys and
sorrows, accomplishments and failures, help us to
keep to the pattern thou hast given us in thy son Jesus
Christ. Amen.

The Meaning of the Cross

> Must Christ still suffer for the world
> Hung on a cross of *gold;*
> Oh, give us wisdom to be strong,
> And courage to be bold.
> —Author Unknown

Scripture: Hebrews 12:11-2; Philippians 2:5-11.

Hymns: "Beneath the Cross of Jesus"; "In the Cross of Christ I Glory."

The Story:

As he preached that morning the distinguished minister of a large church noted the strange attitude of his congregation. The people did not settle down to their usual tolerant attention. The older brothers and sisters did not close their eyes. Many meaningful looks and sibilant whispers were passing around among the assembled members of his church. This continued until the end of the service, and only when he advanced to the altar to dedicate the offerings did he see what had caused the consternation. The cross was not on the altar.

After the service the minister questioned the faithful custodian of the building, who answered: "When I did the final dusting earlier this morning the cross was in its place."

76

The president of the woman's society was greatly perturbed, because she had been on the committee which helped select the cross. She knew that it had been a gift of a wealthy family in the community, and she worried lest they hear of the loss. They might even attend church, as they did on rare occasions, before it was found.

Finally the chairman of the official board decided to call a meeting for the next evening to consider what could be done about it. There was, for once, a good attendance of members. One by one they expressed their suspicions and fears. They all agreed that the expensive cross could be replaced only with great difficulty.

One brother, more timid than the rest, had not expressed himself. His head was bowed and he seemed in deep thought—or was it prayer? As the meeting was about to close without any solution to the problem, he stood up to speak.

"Friends, I have a confession to make—I hid the cross."

A gasp of astonishment came from the lips of everyone in the room.

"Yes," he went on quietly, "Sunday morning early I came to church and entered the sanctuary. After our minister's sermon a few Sundays ago about the meaning of the cross, I wanted to sit and look up at the cross on our altar and try to grasp its meaning to our church and to me. And as I looked I saw it as the symbol of one who had accepted a shameful death that we might know how much he loved us. I saw the early Christians accepting the cross as a symbol and turning it into a sign of sacrifice and redemption. I

wondered just how much it meant to us in our
church. Did our cross mean sacrifice and redemption,
or was it just a part of the beautiful decoration of our
sanctuary? So," repeated the little man, "I hid the
cross until I could find out."

"You hid the cross!" shouted the chairman, as
everyone looked stunned.

The minister arose. "It is my fault," he said humbly,
"I have not sufficiently stressed the spiritual message.
We are privileged to have a beautiful church which
many people and several generations have provided
for us. We have sometimes accepted beauty and order
for true godliness. My sermon on the cross was a
feeble attempt to help us understand its meaning.
Brother Smith has sensed this. Let us pray."

Rows of men and women sat silently with bowed
heads as the minister opened the gates of glory to
them. Then quietly he closed with the Lord's prayer.

"Next Sunday," he stated, "the cross will be on the
altar of our church. May it now be a symbol to us
by which we truly remember our Christ."

THE LOST CHRIST

Your skill has fashioned stately creeds,
  But where is He, we pray—
The friendly Christ of loving deeds?
  He is not here today.

With sentences that twist and tease,
  Confusing mind and heart,
You forge your wordy homilies
  And bid us heed your art.

But where is He—or can you tell?—
  Who stilled the brothers' strife,

Who urged the woman at the well
  To live a better life?

Where is the Saint of Galilee,
  Crude Peter's faithful guide;
The man who wept at Bethany
  Because His friend had died?

We weary of your musty lore
  Behind dead walls of gray;
We want His loving words once more
  By some Emmaus way.

Give us the Christ who can bestow
  Some comfort-thought of death.
Give us a Christ our hearts can know—
  The Man of Nazareth.
                    —THOMAS CURTIS CLARK [26]

PRAYER:

We are tempted to interpret the lessons of life in
easy terms but we learn that life's richest meaning
comes from those experiences which call for strength
and self-control. We thank thee for times of rejoicing
and times of depression. We remember that Christ
came to his glory by way of the cross, and we have
the faith to believe that thou canst give us strength and
power to overcome ourselves and to understand thee.
In Jesus' name. Amen.

Mother Love

The love of a mother is never exhausted. It never changes, it never tires. It endures through all; in good repute, in bad repute, in the face of the world's condemnation. A mother's love still lives on.

—Washington Irving

Scripture: Proverbs 1:8-9; 23:22.

Hymns: "Happy the Home When God Is There"; "O Happy Home, Where Thou Art Loved the Dearest"; "Home, Sweet Home."

The Story:

Once there was a little girl playing about the house by her mother's side. As she was very small, her mother tied her to the string of her apron.

"Little daughter," she said, "when you stumble you can pull yourself up by my apron strings. Thus you will not fall."

The little girl played about happily close to her mother's side. But one day when she had grown so tall that she could look out of the window she stood close to her mother as she washed the glass. Far away the green trees were budding and the flowing river flashed in the sun. The peak of a tall mountain seemed to beckon from the distance.

"Oh, mother," she cried, "untie the apron string and let me go!"

The mother sighed. "Not yet, my child, for yesterday you stumbled and would have fallen but for the apron string. Just wait until you are stronger."

So the child waited and her mother still sang at her work. But one day the girl found the door of young womanhood standing open and it was spring. She looked out upon the world—the trees waved to her, the river sparkled in the sunlight, and the faraway mountain beckoned. She started forth eagerly, and as she went the string of her mother's apron broke.

"How frail is my mother's apron string," she cried gaily, running out into the world with the broken string hanging beside her.

The mother gathered up the other end and treasured it. She went on with her work, not singing but with prayer upon her lips. The girl ran happily on, rejoicing in freedom. She crossed the valley and followed the river. Coming to the foothills she noticed that the river flowed more swiftly and beat against its rock-lined banks. At first the climbing was easy, then steep and rocky, but always as she looked up the lofty peaks beckoned her on.

For many days she climbed and one day found herself on the brink of a precipice. The river foamed and flashed over it and the mist filled her eyes. She could not see, grew dizzy, stumbled, and would have fallen over the precipice to her death had not something about her caught on a point of a rock at the very edge, and there she hung dangling. She put her hand up to hold the rock which had caught her and found she was held by the broken string of her mother's apron.

"How strong is my mother's apron string," she cried

as she drew herself up and stood safe again. Leaving the precipice she walked toward the peaks in the distance.[27]

APRON STRINGS

I'm all tied up in ventures
   Into worldly sort of things,
But the ties that bind me tightest
   Are my mother's apron strings.
Whenever I may stray a bit
   I feel them tugging still,
And straining hard to hold me back;
   I guess they always will.

Oh, apron strings are heart strings
   And never come untied.
They're woven from the wool of life,
   Defying time and tide.
Though broken are most ties that bind
   Us to the days long past,
We cannot break these strings of love
   That ever hold us fast.

They span the years and stretch for miles
   But never loose their hold
Upon the hearts of all of us,
   No matter young or old;
And when we're drifting down the Styx,
   These apron strings, once more,
Like life lines thrown across a wreck,
   Will bring us safe to shore.

—BERT BARON

PRAYER:

O gracious Lord, who wast born of a woman, who didst accept the ministry of woman, and who didst take into thine arms little children to bless them, be very present with us during this hour. Be with all to whom thou hast given the care of children, that these may be guided and guarded during tender years and led gently in the paths of righteousness. Help those of us who have mothers to inspire us, to understand the deep yearnings of their hearts, and lend to us all the light of thy presence and the joy of thy peace. Hear us for thy name's sake. Amen.

The New Year

Yesterday the year was old and tired
And beaten hard with frequent travel.
To and fro we went in weary repetition
Of old familiar ways and deeds.
Today the year is young and clean,
Like freshly fallen snow,
The ruts and scars are gone,
And we are called to new and brave adventure.
—Lucius H. Bugbee [23]

Scripture: II Corinthians 3:2-6.

Hymn: "O God, Our Help in Ages Past."

RECIPE FOR A GOOD NEW YEAR

Take twelve fine, full-grown months; see that these are thoroughly free from all the old memories of bitterness, rancor, hate, and jealousy. Cleanse them completely from every clinging spite, pick off all specks of pettiness and littleness; in short, see that these months are free from all the past. Have them as fresh and clean as when they first came out of the storehouse of time. Cut these months into thirty or thirty-one equal parts. This batch will keep for just one year. Do not attempt to make up the whole batch at one time, as so many persons spoil it in this way, but prepare one day at a time as follows:

Into each day put twelve parts of faith, eleven parts of patience, ten of courage, nine of work (some people omit this ingredient and spoil the rest), eight of hope, seven of fidelity, six of liberty, five of kindness, four of rest (leaving this out is like leaving oil out of the salad—don't do it), three of prayer, two of meditation, and one well-selected resolution. Put in about one tablespoon of good spirits, a dash of fun, a sprinkling of play, and a heaping cupful of good humor. Pour into the whole a liberal amount of love, and mix with a vim. Cook thoroughly in a fervent heat, garnish with a few smiles, and a sprig of joy. Then serve with quietness, unselfishness, and cheerfulness, and a happy New Year is a certainty.[29]

THE STORY:

It was the last evening of the old year, and I sat watching the little flame dancing upon the logs I had piled in the fireplace. The room was in the shadow except for the light which came from the hearth. Suddenly I was aware that I was no longer alone. A tall and stately figure stood looking at me. He was hooded and cloaked with a fabric somewhat like mist. His face was pure and kind and as I looked into his eyes, I saw the storied panorama of the past.

I said, very softly, "Who are you?"

And he answered simply, "I am Time."

"But," I exclaimed, "the cartoonists picture you as a bald old fellow with whiskers and carrying a scythe."

"I am surprised that you get your ideas of life from the cartoonists," he answered, "and, incidently, I have no use for a scythe. Most people mow themselves down with scythes of their own invention and follies."

I noticed that his garment seemed to be of many shades. There were patches on it like great ink spots and occasional splashes of gorgeous color. Answering my unspoken thought, he said: "The dark tints you see in my dress are the cruelties and stupidities of men. This old spot represents a crucifixion in Judea, and this newer splotch is the war to end war. Two fresh stains upon me are the lawlessness which frets these days. This golden place is for the sacrificial gifts of the loving poor, and this touch of glory is for the dedications of great leadership. Virtues brighten my robes and sins darken it. I can wear only what men give me."

"Thank you for telling me," I said. "Your dress might be darker than it is."

"Yes," he answered, "and brighter."

I looked at the clock and saw that but two minutes remained of the old year. So I sat up straight and said: "Tell me quickly; do we human beings amount to much in this vast jumble of stars and mud?"

"More than you think," was his reply. "Stars are your footlights and mud your stage, but you are the drama."

This was getting somewhere, I thought, so I tried him again; "What is going to happen, for instance, to me?"

"That all depends on you," he answered.

I was annoyed, and muttered impatiently; "Copybook stuff!" He looked at me sternly: "The trouble with your generation is that you laugh at copybook maxims. Some good things you had to write over and over again, like 'Procrastination is the thief of time.' Do not forget them."

The anguish of separation was upon me: "But what about those I love? People plunge so easily into shame and failure. What can I do?"

"Well," he answered, "you human beings are all in the same process. You can help each other if you will only use your heads—and your hearts."

I looked at the clock. The minute hand hovered on twelve, so I said breathlessly: "When will I be through with time?"

He considered for a moment and I saw that he knew, but he shook his head finally and said: "What does it matter?"

He turned to go, but I cried: "Wait! one thing more. Is it all right on ahead?"

He smiled and my heart warmed. Then factory whistles blew, shots were fired in the street, a new year had come and Father Time vanished.[30]

A NEW START

I will start anew this morning with a higher, fairer creed;
I will cease to stand complaining of my ruthless neighbor's greed;
I will cease to sit repining while my duty's call is clear;
I will waste no moment whining, and my heart shall know no fear.

I will look sometimes about me for the things that merit praise;
I will search for hidden beauties that elude the grumbler's gaze.
I will try to find contentment in the paths that I must tread;
I will cease to have resentment when another moves ahead.

I will not be swayed by envy when my rival's strength is shown;
I will not deny his merit, but I'll strive to prove my own;
I will try to see the beauty spread before me, rain or shine;
I will cease to preach your duty, and be more concerned with mine.

—Author Unknown

PRAYER FOR THE NEW YEAR:

I would bring unto thee, O Lord and Master, the mistakes and follies of the year that has gone. I bring into thy sight the words that wounded, the thoughts that befouled, the deeds that degraded, the purposes that centered in myself, and all the unholy brood of jealousies, envies, malice, spites, and hates. In shame and penitence I look upon them for the last time and turn from them to the promise of a year that is new and clean. I thank thee for the splendor of the unstained future. I thank thee for the opportunity to do what I have failed to do. I rejoice in the tang of new tasks. I am grateful for the hope of the un-turned page. I would, O God, dedicate myself anew to the clean life; to the loving and unselfish spirit; to the cheer and good will that are needed by other hearts; to the love of good books; the choosing and holding of genuine friends; to thy will; and to the establish-ment of thy Kingdom in this thy world. Hold me steady when these purposes prove difficult to retain. Grant me the grace of thy presence along the way. And save me from despair in the hour of my defeat. Amen.[81]

One Step at a Time

Never bear more than one trouble at a time. Some people bear three kinds—all they have ever had, all they have now, and all they expect to have.

—Edward Everett Hale

Scripture: Matthew 6:34; Luke 12:22-26.

Hymns: "Lord, for Tomorrow and Its Needs"; "Lead, Kindly Light."

LOOK TO THIS DAY

Look to this day!
For it is life, the very life of life.
In its brief course lie all the varieties and realities of your
    existence:
The bliss of growth;
The glory of action;
The splendor of beauty;
For yesterday is already a dream, and tomorrow is only a
    vision;
But today, well lived, makes every yesterday
A dream of happiness, and every tomorrow a vision of
    hope.
Look well, therefore, to this day!
Such is the salutation of the dawn!

—From the Sanskrit

The Story:

The pendulum on the clock had been swinging for a long, long time. Occasionally it would get a little

89

tired, and the master of the house would wind it
and the pendulum would swing merrily again.

It seemed such a happy thing to do, when it was
first wound—to swing evenly to and fro. But on the
last of the old year the glass door on the clock said
to the pendulum: "You are not getting anywhere, just
swinging from side to side. You might as well remain
quiet as I do. How do you know you will have the
strength to swing the thousands of times necessary for
next year?" He talked thus all day long and the
pendulum grew worried.

On New Year's Eve the pendulum stopped. He
counted what he had done during the last year and
discovered that he had swung back and forth 31,-
536,000 times. He decided he couldn't swing through
another year—the task was much too great. When the
master of the house came along, he chided the silent
clock and pendulum.

"No one could expect me to swing 31,536,000
times," complained the culprit.

"Certainly not," said the master. "That would be
too much for anyone. But surely you can swing once
in a second, that is all I ask of you." He wound the
clock once more.

The pendulum took heart. He proceeded to swing
just once in a second. It was easy. He swung again—
it was just as easy. And so he went on happily through
the year. At the end of it, he had swung exactly
31,536,000 times, yet he was not tired.

PRAYER:

> For this one day alone, dear God, I pray;
> Help me to walk the straight and narrow way
>   With cheerful mind;
> Help me to think, to act, the Golden Rule,
> To do my best with book or beast or tool,
>   To serve mankind.
>
> Help me to think before I speak a word
> That might, by chance, hurt one who overheard,
>   And make him sad;
> Help me to laugh with clean and wholesome mirth,
> To scorn the thought that evil minds give birth,
>   Or actions bad.
>
> Help me to see in sunshine and in rain,
> In daylight and in dark, Thy hand again,
>   Thy love alone;
> And then at eve, when work is put away,
> Help me, dear Lord, to lift my eyes and say,
>   "Thy will be done."
>
> —MARGARET RUTHERFORD [32]

The Tithe

> The spirit of self-sacrifice
> Stays not to count the price.
> Christ did not of his mere abundance cast
> Into the empty treasury of man's store;
> The First and Last
> Gave until he could give no more;
> His very living,
> Such was Christ's giving.
>
> —Anna E. Hamilton

Scripture: Leviticus 27:30-32; Genesis 28:20-22; Malachi 3:7-12; John 3:27.

Hymns: "Take My Life, and Let It Be"; "We Give Thee but Thine Own."

The Story:

It was autumn and the country church stood forlornly by the side of the road. Around it was a prosperous farming community. But the church needed painting. Several window panes were cracked, the steeple needed mending, and the front steps were broken down.

All this could be seen from the road, but when one entered the church itself it was evident that it had had little care for several years. Only a handful of people turned out for services on the fourth Sunday when the preacher came. He always seemed disheartened when he did arrive and the congregation did little to revive him.

Finally the faithful few met to decide the fate of the church. It had been on the highway for many years and had at one time been beloved and a place of activity. It seemed now as if it would be abandoned. After everyone else had spoken, and no one had a plan to save the church, the miller stood up.

"I don't like to see this church deserted," he said. "My boys grew up here and they are both Christian laymen in the towns where they live. Furthermore, we need the influence of the church. Many children are in the community and we should have a big Sunday school too. The women enjoy getting together and need a nice room. We need a men's club, and young and old ought to have a meeting place for worship every Sunday. I have a plan to keep it going and to get the things we need. But don't ask me how. Just say the word, watch the church, and keep coming every Sunday. Get others to come and in one year I'll explain my plan."

Well, the little group thought that was an easy solution, and as they hated to lock the doors of the church, they agreed that whatever plan the miller had would be all right.

The next Sunday it was noticed that the steps were mended, the cracked windows replaced, and the weeds cut down. Every week something was done—the church was painted, the steeple mended, new hymn books and Bibles appeared, there were inside decorations, a new carpet, and finally a piano was added. It was difficult for the members of the church to refrain from asking the miller about his plan, but when they did, he merely smiled and passed the time of day. The mystery of it brought many people to the church and they liked it so well that they came back. A choir was organized and it practiced regularly with a director who was proud to give his time.

The young folks started to attend church and asked to have a meeting every Sunday night for themselves. New lighting fixtures than appeared and a suitable leader's table. The preacher got a new black suit. One happy day the women came together and cleaned the room at the side of the church so that they could meet there regularly. A men's club was formed and they kept the grass cut and the trees pruned. The little church by the side of the road was no more forlorn but a happy meeting place for everyone in of the community.

When the twelve months had rolled around everyone crowded into the church to learn how the miller had gotten the money to make all the improvements. After a devotional period, the minister called upon the miller to speak.

"Well," said he, "you did all of this yourselves— that is, you paid for it."

"How?" they cried, "you didn't ask us for a cent."

"When you brought your grain to my mill to be ground, I took out the Lords tenth and gave you back the nine tenths," he said. "I sold it and with the money and with my own tithe honored God's house and paid the minister."

They crowded around him and everyone was happy. But he had not finished yet!

"How many of you missed the tenth?" he asked. No one answered. "Then I move that we have a full-

time minister and that we continue to give our tenth
to the work of the Kingdom."

There was no dissenting vote.

THE MINIMUM STANDARD OF GIVING

I believe in the tithe as the minimum standard of giving
for all Christian people. I believe it has the approval of
Jesus. I believe anything less has his disapproval. I believe it has the approval of human experience. I believe
it is the gateway into the larger sense of stewardship. I
believe its practice will prove a means of grace, just as
prayer, Bible reading, and church attendance. I further
believe that any church which neglects to emphasize the
benefits of tithing both to the individual and to the
Kingdom of human needs has failed to do its duty.[33]

PRAYER:

O God, our Father, thou dost read our hearts; help
us to increase our spending for things eternal. Help
us to count all things but loss to win thee, who art
wealth inexhaustible. We thank thee for the good
things of life, for continual touch with the divine,
for all lessons of experience, and for the steps by which
we climb to higher things. Teach us how to be
allied to the infinite and yet respond to human needs.
In Jesus' name. Amen.

The Value of the Bible

> We search the world for truth. We cull
> The good, the true, the beautiful,
> From graven stone and written scroll,
> And all old flower-fields of the soul;
> And, weary seekers of the best,
> We come back laden from our quest,
> To find that all the sages said
> In in the Book our mothers read.
> —JOHN GREENLEAF WHITTIER

SCRIPTURE: John I 1-5; Isaiah 55:1-3.

HYMNS: "Break Thou the Bread of Life"; "O Word of God Incarnate."

MEDITATION:

Born in the East, and clothed in Oriental form and imagery, the Bible walks the ways of the world with familiar feet, and enters land after land to find its own everywhere. It has learned to speak in hundreds of languages to the heart of man. It comes into the palace, to tell the monarch that he is the servant of the Most High, and into the cottage to assure the peasant that he is the son of God. Children listen to its stories with wonder and delight, and wise men ponder them as parables of life. It has a word of peace for the time of peril, a word of comfort for the day of calamity, a word of light for the hour of darkness. Its oracles are repeated in the assemblies of the people, and its counsels whispered in the ear of the lonely. The wise and the proud tremble at its warnings, but to the wounded and penitent it has a mothers voice. The wilderness and the solitary place have been made glad by it, and the fire on the hearth has lighted the reading of its well-worn pages. It has woven itself into our deepest affections, and colored our dearest dreams; so that love and friendship, sympathy and devotion, memory and hope, put on the beautiful garments of its treasured speech, breathing of frankincense and myrrh. Above the cradle and beside the grave its great words come to us uncalled. They fill our prayers with power larger than we know, and the beauty of them lingers in our ears long after the sermons which have been forgotten. They return to us swiftly and quietly, like birds flying from far away. They surprise us with new meanings, like springs of water breaking forth from the mountain beside a long-forgotten path. They grow richer, as pearls do when they are worn near the heart. No man is poor or desolate who has this treasure for his own. When the landscape darkens and the trembling pilgrim comes to the Valley named of the Shadow, he is not afraid to enter: he takes the rod and staff of Scriptures in his hand; he says to friend and comrade: "Good-by, we shall meet again"; and comforted by that support, he goes toward the lonely pass as one walks through darkness into light.[84]

THE BIBLE

When I am tired, the Bible is my bed;
Or in the dark, the Bible is my light;

When I am hungry, it is vital bread;
Or fearful, it is armor for the fight.
When I am sick, 'tis healing medicine;
Or lonely, thronging friends I find therein.

If I would work, the Bible is my tool;
Or play, it is a harp of happy sound.
If I am ignorant, it is my school;
If I am sinking, it is solid ground.
And wings, if boldly I aspire.

Should I be lost, the Bible is my guide;
Or naked, it is raiment, rich and warm.
Am I imprisoned, it is ranges wide;
Or tempest-tossed, a shelter from the storm.
Would I adventure, 'tis a gallant sea.

Does gloom oppress? The Bible is a sun.
Or ugliness? It is a garden fair.

—AUTHOR UNKNOWN

PRAYER:

Gracious Father, each day brings us fresh revelations of thee and thy power. We thank thee for the Scriptures and for thy wisdom. Help us to get the lessons thou dost teach through the lives of all who have tried to walk in thy way. As in the days of old men walked with Jesus and thereby found fellowship with thee, may we today walk with him who went about doing good. May we comprehend more clearly the blessedness of fellowship and claim more fully thy promise to thy children. Amen.

Willing Service

> I never cut my neighbors throat;
>   My neighbors gold I never stole;
> I never spoiled his house and land,
>   But God have mercy on my soul!
>
> For I am haunted night and day
>   By all the deeds I have not done!
> —Marguerite Wilkinson [85]

SCRIPTURE: Romans 12:1-18.

HYMN: "O Master, Let Me Walk With Thee."

THE STORY:

Once upon a time a king grew weary of the carelessness of his people. They were continually neglecting the small things which might make the great tasks easy. He decided he would find out if there was a man of vision among them. One day, carrying a bag of gold, he secretly went to the main road leading past his palace. After digging a hole he placed the bag of gold therein, but instead of covering it he rolled a huge stone over it. On the bag of gold he had written: "The one who finds this bag may keep it." Then he went home to watch from his window.

Many people passed in carts, on foot, and on horseback. The pedestrians walked around the side of the stone, the horsemen pulled their steeds up and directed them also around the stone, and the men in carts made

99

a new track on the hillside, almost upsetting their
vehicles to avoid the stone. But no one had the time
or the courtesy to roll the stone away.

When a company of soldiers marched along they
broke rank in order to file by it, and the stone still lay
in the middle of the road. This went on for many days
and everyone wondered who had placed the obstruction on the road. They were quite upset about it.

Finally after several weeks the king invited all the
people of the countryside to meet him at the stone.
When they assembled he easily rolled the obstruction
to the side of the road disclosing the hole in which lay
the bag of gold.

"You have been wondering who placed this stone
in the middle of the road. I was the culprit, but I also
placed this treasure for the one who would clear it
away. Daily you have passed by with no thought for
the ones who might follow you or for your own future
ease." He then untied the bag and the golden coins
poured out.

JESUS CHRIST—AND WE

Christ has no hands but our hands
    To do his work today;
He has no feet but our feet
    To lead men in his way;
He has no tongue but our tongues
    To tell men how he died;
He has no help but our help
    To bring them to his side.

We are the only Bible
    The careless world will read;
We are the sinner's gospel,

We are the scoffer's creed;
We are the Lord's last message
　Given in deed and word—
What if the line is crooked?
　What if the type is blurred?

What if our hands are busy
　With other work than his?
What if our feet are walking
　Where sin's allurement is?
What if our tongues are speaking
　Of things his lips would spurn?
How can we hope to help him
　Unless from him we learn?
　　　　　—ANNIE JOHNSON FLINT [36]

OPPORTUNITY

They do me wrong who say I come no more
　When once I knock and fail to find you in;
For every day I stand outside your door
　And bid you wake, and rise to fight and win.
　　　　　—WALTER MALONE

PRAYER:

O God, we thank thee for the men and women of other days and of our own times who have loyally served humanity. Today there are still foes of human progress and enemies of the common good to be overcome. May we not shirk our tasks, in this day, nor be discouraged. Help us to be confident that truth and right shall triumph and to work forcefully with thee to bring thy Kingdom on earth. Amen.

You Live as You Think

Lord take away from me fear thoughts that cloud my days,
And let me move serene to meet life's every phase.
Blot fear from out my mind and let my soul be clear
Of it forevermore, nor feel its presence near.
—GEORGE ELLISTON [87]

SCRIPTURE: Philippians 2:4-11; 4:8.

HYMN: "Take Time to Be Holy."

THE STORY:

Once upon a time a woman was given a beautiful home. It had all the lovely things in it and around it to make one happy.

Strange as it may seem, as soon as she moved in she drew the blinds tightly. The sunlight of God's love never entered the spacious rooms again.

More shocking than this, she brought with her trunks full of worn-out draperies, cushions, and rugs. These she threw over the beautiful furnishings of the house.

Each day when she went out she gathered trash and refuse, depositing it in the living room. Rags, bottles, and bones, symbolic of murder and crime filled the classic bookcases. She never dusted or swept down cobwebs from her walls. The furniture and hangings of the house soon looked shabby and dirty.

When she first moved into the house a few callers

appeared. Though she invited them to come in they were forced to sit on the ragged coverings she had placed over the finely upholstered furniture. She talked incessantly, calling attention to the horrible things with which she was surrounded. The callers stopped coming.

She would often walk about the house saying: "What a sorry place in which to live. The world is growing worse and worse."

Sitting down at her desk she wrote many a sharp note of criticism, blaming many people for as many misdemeanors, and, of course, signing no name to the communications.

As she walked about her bedroom at night (of course she seldom slept) she went over in her mind the snubs and slights she had received from childhood and held them tenderly close to her heart, together with the discarded dresses and broken toys of her former days.

What satisfaction she got from life is beyond understanding! [33]

THE GLOW WITHIN

Oh, you gotta get a glory
   In the work you do:
A hallelujah chorus
   In the heart of you.
Paint or tell a story,
   Sing or shovel coal;
You gotta get a glory
   Or your job lacks soul.

The great, whose shining labors
   Make our pulses throb,
Were men who gotta glory
   In their daily job.

The battle might be gory
   And the odds unfair,
But the men who gotta **glory**
   Never knew despair.

To those who gotta glory
   It is like the sun,
And you can see it glowing
   Through the work they've done.
Oh, fame is transitory
   Riches fade away,
But when you gotta glory
   It is there to stay.

Oh, Lord, give me a **glory**,
   Is it much to give?
For you gotta get a glory
   Or you just don't live!
Oh, Lord, give me a glory,
   And a workman's pride
For you gotta get a glory
   Or you're dead inside!
               —BERTON BRALEY [39]

PRAYER:

O God, our Father, help us to master ourselves. May we this day have reverence for goodness, truth, and beauty. In our contacts with others help us to have the spirit of courtesy and good will. May we forget all bitterness and prejudice, taking what thou dost give us of joy and beauty with a glad and thankful heart. And then add the joy of willing, unthanked service and a glory within. In Jesus' name. Amen.

References

1. From *Hail, Man!* By permission of Dodd, Mead & Co., Inc.
2. From "God's Dreams." By permission of Thomas Curtis Clark.
3. Adapted from "The Black Madonna," in *Merry-Go-Round*, by Margaret T. Applegarth. Copyright 1925 by The Judson Press.
4. By permission of Grace Noll Crowell.
5. "The World Is Full of Children." By permission of Nancy Byrd Turner.
6. By permission of Harry Emerson Fosdick.
7. From "A King Might Miss the Guiding Star." By permisson of Mrs. Robert F. Jefferys.
8. "Christmas Eve, 1941." By permission of the *Christian Advocate*.
9. From *Bound in the Bundle of Life*. By permission of the publisher, Harper & Brothers.
10. Adapted from "The Man Who Was Too Busy to Find the Child" by permission of the author, Lucius H. Bugbee.
11. By permission of Ruby Dell Baugher and the *Christian Herald*.
12. By Toyohiko Kagawa.
13. From "And a Little Child Shall Lead Them." By permission of Clyde McGee.
14. Adapted from a story in a lecture by Hugh Price Hughes.
15. Prayer of Francis of Assisi.
16. From "In the Soul's Windows." By permission of Marion Lee and the *Christian Herald*.
17. From *Songs of the Average Man*, by Sam Walter Foss. Copyright 1907. By permission of Lothrop, Lee & Shepard Co., New York.

18. By permission of Thomas Curtis Clark.

19. Adapted from "Growing Toward God," in *More Fireside Stories for Girls in Their Teens,* by permission of the author, Margaret Eggleston Owen, and the publisher, Harper & Brothers.

20. By permission of Mary Dickerson Bangham and *Parents' Magazine.*

21. Adapted from *The Golden Windows* by Laura E. Richards. Copyright 1903 by Little, Brown & Co. Reprinted by permission of Little, Brown & Co.

22. From "Gratitude." By permission of Clyde McGee.

23. From "Earth's Common Things." By permission of the author's son, the Rev. Maxwell Savage.

24. "My Tapestry." By permission of Adah Lyle Kidder.

25. Author unknown.

26. By permission of Thomas Curtis Clark.

27. Adapted from *The Golden Windows* by Laura E. Richards. Copyright 1903 by Little, Brown & Co. Reprinted by permission of Little, Brown & Co.

28. By permission of Lucius H. Bugbee.

29. By permission of the *P.E.O. Record.*

30. "An Interview with Father Time." By permission of the author, Samuel Harkness, and the *Christian Century.*

31. By permission of Percy R. Hayward.

32. By permission of the *United Church Observer.*

33. By permission of the General Board of Lay Activities of The Methodist Church.

34. Author unknown.

35. From "Guilty." Used by permission.

36. Copyright. Reprinted by permission of Evangelical Publishers, Toronto, Canada.

37. From *Everyday Poems.* By permission of Stewart Kidd, Cincinnati.

38. Adapted from a story by W. V. Meredith.

39. By permission of Berton Braley. Copyright by Curtis Publishing Company.